T0084250

PIANO SOLO

WINTER
SOLSTICE

ISBN 978-1-4803-3768-8

HAL•LEONARD®
CORPORATION

7777 W. BLUEMOUND RD. P.O. BOX 13819 MILWAUKEE, WI 53213

Visit Hal Leonard Online at
www.halleonard.com

CONTENTS

Babe Is Born/Enter the Stable Gently

Traditional Spanish Song
Arranged by Liz Story

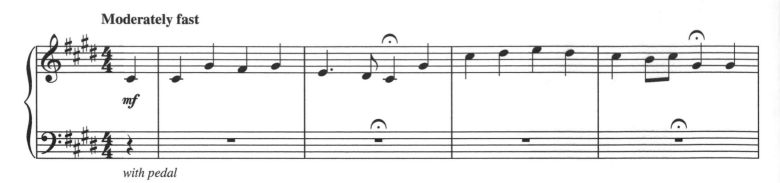

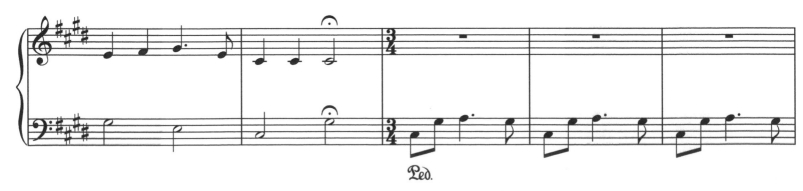

D.S. al Coda

Coda

rit.

a tempo

rit.

By the Fireside

By Allaudin Mathieu

Moderately, somewhat freely

with pedal

9

Carol of the Bells

Words and Music by
Michael Jones

Christmas Hymn

Words and Music by
Billy Childs

Moderately slow, in 2; somewhat freely

mf

with pedal

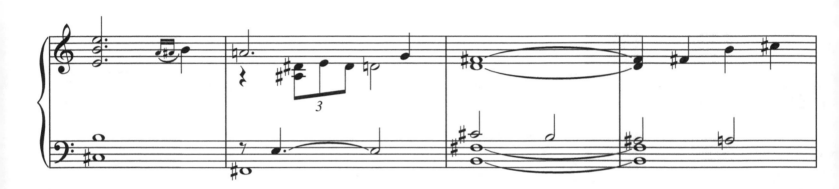

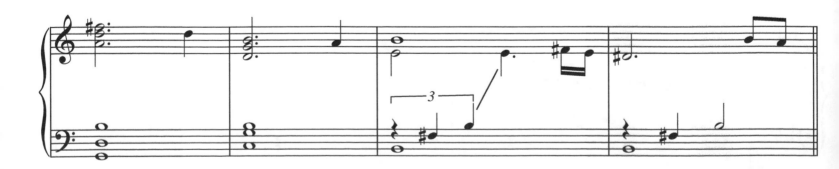

Christmas Time Is Here

from A CHARLIE BROWN CHRISTMAS

Words by Lee Mendelson

Music by Vince Guaraldi

The Gift

By Philip Aaberg

Happy Xmas

(War Is Over)

Written by
John Lennon and Yoko Ono

Moderately fast

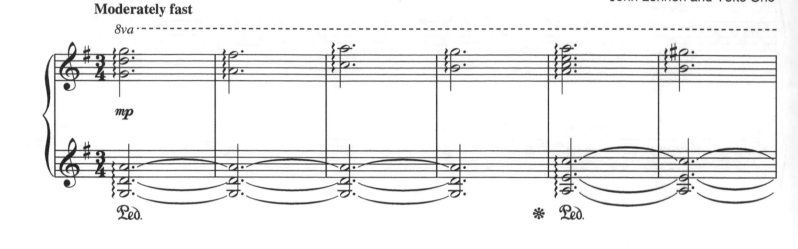

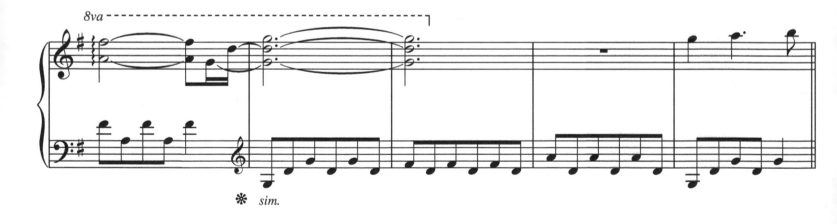

High Plains

By Philip Aaberg

The Holly & the Ivy

Traditional
Arranged by David Lanz

The Homecoming

Music by John Tesh

Hopeful

By Michael Manring

a tempo

8va -

rit. e dim.

p

Ped.

✻

Joy to the World

Traditional
Arranged by Jim Brickman

O Come Little Children/
We'll Dress the House

O COME LITTLE CHILDREN
German Carol
Music by Peter Schulz (1790)
Arranged by Liz Story

WE'LL DRESS THE HOUSE
Lyric by Wihla Hutson
Music by Alfred Burt

Brightly

*Play cue notes 2nd time only.

A Quiet Time

By Jim Brickman

Moderately slow; gently, freely

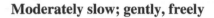

Shades of White

Words and Music by
Jim Brickman

Shepherd's Rocking Carol

By Philip Aaberg

Moderately, somewhat freely

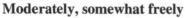
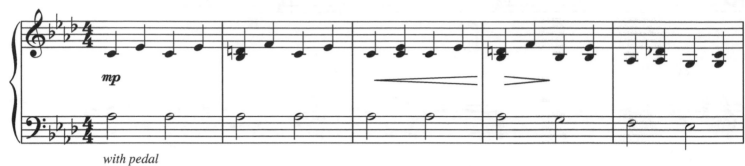

Silent Night

Traditional
Arranged by Jim Brickman

Snowfall

By Liz Story

To Coda

D.S. al Coda

Coda

What Child Is This

Words and Music by
David Lanz

Gently

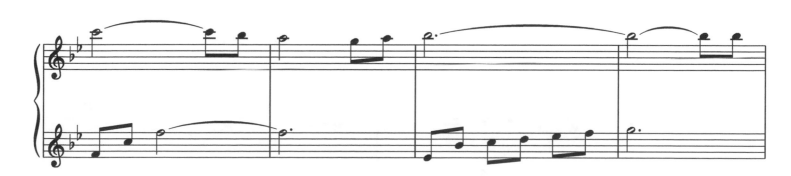

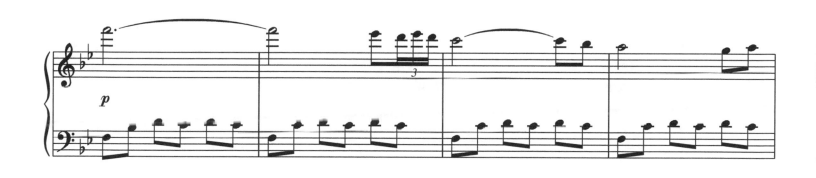

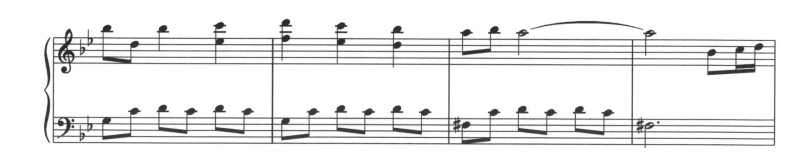

Slower

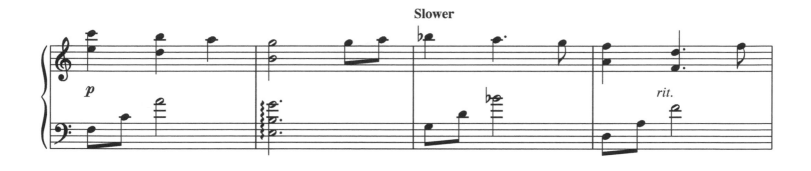

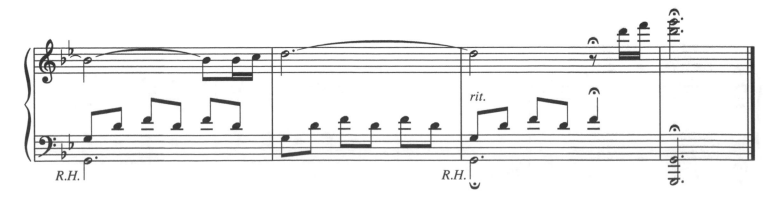

YOUR FAVORITE MUSIC
ARRANGED FOR PIANO SOLO

ADELE FOR PIANO SOLO – 2ND EDITION

This collection features 13 Adele favorites beautifully arranged for piano solo, including: Chasing Pavements • Hello • Rolling in the Deep • Set Fire to the Rain • Someone like You • Turning Tables • When We Were Young • and more.

00307585 ....$14.99

PRIDE & PREJUDICE

12 piano pieces from the 2006 Oscar-nominated film, including: Another Dance • Darcy's Letter • Georgiana • Leaving Netherfield • Liz on Top of the World • Meryton Townhall • The Secret Life of Daydreams • Stars and Butterflies • and more.

00313327 ....$17.99

BATTLESTAR GALACTICA
by Bear McCreary

For this special collection, McCreary himself has translated the acclaimed orchestral score into fantastic solo piano arrangements at the intermediate to advanced level. Includes 19 selections in all, and as a bonus, simplified versions of "Roslin and Adama" and "Wander My Friends." Contains a note from McCreary, as well as a biography.

00313530 ....$17.99

GEORGE GERSHWIN – RHAPSODY IN BLUE (ORIGINAL)
Alfred Publishing Co.

George Gershwin's own piano solo arrangement of his classic contemporary masterpiece for piano and orchestra. This masterful measure-for-measure two-hand adaptation of the complete modern concerto for piano and orchestra incorporates all orchestral parts and piano passages into two staves while retaining the clarity, sonority, and brilliance of the original.

00321589 ....$16.99

THE BEST JAZZ PIANO SOLOS EVER

Over 300 pages of beautiful classic jazz piano solos featuring standards in any jazz artist's repertoire. Includes: Afternoon in Paris • Giant Steps • Moonlight in Vermont • Moten Swing • A Night in Tunisia • Night Train • On Green Dolphin Street • Song for My Father • West Coast Blues • Yardbird Suite • and more.

00312079 ....$19.99

ROMANTIC FILM MUSIC

40 piano solo arrangements of beloved songs from the silver screen, including: Anyone at All • Come What May • Glory of Love • I See the Light • I Will Always Love You • Iris • It Had to Be You • Nobody Does It Better • She • Take My Breath Away (Love Theme) • A Thousand Years • Up Where We Belong • When You Love Someone • The Wind Beneath My Wings • and many more.

00122112 ....$17.99

CLASSICS WITH A TOUCH OF JAZZ
Arranged by Lee Evans

27 classical masterpieces arranged in a unique and accessible jazz style. Mr Evans also provides an audio recording of each piece. Titles include: Air from Suite No. 3 (Bach) • Barcarolle "June" (Tchaikovsky) • Pavane (Faure) • Piano Sonata No. 8 "Pathetique" (Beethoven) • Reverie (Debussy) • The Swan (Saint-Saens) • and more.

00151662 Book/Online Audio..$14.99

STAR WARS: THE FORCE AWAKENS

Music from the soundtrack to the seventh installment of the Star Wars® franchise by John Williams is presented in this songbook, complete with artwork from the film throughout the whole book, including eight pages in full color! Titles include: The Scavenger • Rey Meets BB-8 • Rey's Theme • That Girl with the Staff • Finn's Confession • The Starkiller • March of the Resistance • Torn Apart • and more.

00154451 ....$17.99

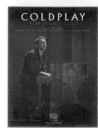

COLDPLAY FOR PIANO SOLO

Stellar solo arrangements of a dozen smash hits from Coldplay: Clocks • Fix You • In My Place • Lost! • Paradise • The Scientist • Speed of Sound • Trouble • Up in Flames • Viva La Vida • What If • Yellow.

00307637 ....$15.99

TAYLOR SWIFT FOR PIANO SOLO – 2ND EDITION

This updated second edition features 15 of Taylor's biggest hits from her self-titled first album all the way through her pop breakthrough album, *1989*. Includes: Back to December • Blank Space • Fifteen • I Knew You Were Trouble • Love Story • Mean • Mine • Picture to Burn • Shake It Off • Teardrops on My Guitar • 22 • We Are Never Ever Getting Back Together • White Horse • Wildest Dreams • You Belong with Me.

00307375 ....$16.99

DISNEY SONGS

12 Disney favorites in beautiful piano solo arrangements, including: Bella Notte (This Is the Night) • Can I Have This Dance • Feed the Birds • He's a Tramp • I'm Late • The Medallion Calls • Once Upon a Dream • A Spoonful of Sugar • That's How You Know • We're All in This Together • You Are the Music in Me • You'll Be in My Heart (Pop Version).

00313527 ....$14.99

UP
Music by Michael Giacchino

Piano solo arrangements of 13 pieces from Pixar's mammoth animated hit: Carl Goes Up • It's Just a House • Kevin Beak'n • Married Life • Memories Can Weigh You Down • The Nickel Tour • Paradise Found • The Small Mailman Returns • The Spirit of Adventure • Stuff We Did • We're in the Club Now • and more, plus a special section of full-color artwork from the film!

00313471 ....$17.99

GREAT THEMES FOR PIANO SOLO

Nearly 30 rich arrangements of popular themes from movies and TV shows, including: Bella's Lullaby • Chariots of Fire • Cinema Paradiso • The Godfather (Love Theme) • Hawaii Five-O Theme • Theme from "Jaws" • Theme from "Jurassic Park" • Linus and Lucy • The Pink Panther • Twilight Zone Main Title • and more.

00312102 ....$14.99

Prices, content, and availability subject to change without notice.
Disney Characters and Artwork TM & © 2018 Disney

7777 W. BLUEMOUND RD. P.O. BOX 13819 MILWAUKEE, WI 53213

www.halleonard.com

CHRISTMAS COLLECTIONS
FROM HAL LEONARD
ALL BOOKS ARRANGED FOR PIANO, VOICE & GUITAR

The Best Christmas Songs Ever – 6th Edition

69 all-time favorites are included in the 6th edition of this collection of Christmas tunes. Includes: Auld Lang Syne • Coventry Carol • Frosty the Snow Man • Happy Holiday • It Came Upon the Midnight Clear • O Holy Night • Rudolph the Red-Nosed Reindeer • Silver Bells • What Child Is This? • and many more.

00359130...$27.50

The Big Book of Christmas Songs – 2nd Edition

An outstanding collection of over 120 all-time Christmas favorites and hard-to-find classics. Features: Angels We Have Heard on High • As Each Happy Christmas • Auld Lang Syne • The Boar's Head Carol • Christ Was Born on Christmas Day • Bring a Torch Jeannette, Isabella • Carol of the Bells • Coventry Carol • Deck the Halls • The First Noel • The Friendly Beasts • God Rest Ye Merry Gentlemen • I Heard the Bells on Christmas Day • It Came Upon a Midnight Clear • Jesu, Joy of Man's Desiring • Joy to the World • Masters in This Hall • O Holy Night • The Story of the Shepherd • 'Twas the Night Before Christmas • What Child Is This? • and many more. Includes guitar chord frames.

00311520...$19.95

Christmas Songs – Budget Books

Save some money this Christmas with this fabulous budget-priced collection of 100 holiday favorites: All I Want for Christmas Is You • Christmas Time Is Here • Feliz Navidad • Grandma Got Run Over by a Reindeer • Happy Holiday • I'll Be Home for Christmas • Jesus Born on This Day • Last Christmas • Merry Christmas, Baby • O Holy Night • Please Come Home for Christmas • Rockin' Around the Christmas Tree • Some Children See Him • We Need a Little Christmas • What Child Is This? • and more.

00310887...$14.99

The Definitive Christmas Collection – 3rd Edition

Revised with even more Christmas classics, this must-have 3rd edition contains 127 top songs, such as: Blue Christmas • Christmas Time Is Here • Do You Hear What I Hear • The First Noel • A Holly Jolly Christmas • Jingle-Bell Rock • Little Saint Nick • Merry Christmas, Darling • O Holy Night • Rudolph, the Red-Nosed Reindeer • Silver and Gold • We Need a Little Christmas • You're All I Want for Christmas • and more!

00311602...$24.95

The Most Requested Christmas Songs

This giant collection features nearly 70 holiday classics, from traditional carols to modern Christmas hits: Blue Christmas • Christmas Time Is Here • Deck the Hall • Feliz Navidad • I'll Be Home for Christmas • Jingle Bells • Little Saint Nick • Nuttin' for Christmas • Rudolph the Red-Nosed Reindeer • Silent Night • and more.

00001563...$19.99

The Muppet Christmas Carol

Matching folio to the blockbuster movie featuring 11 Muppet carols and eight pages of color photos. Bless Us All • Chairman of the Board • Christmas Scat • Finale - When Love Is Found/It Feels like Christmas • It Feels like Christmas • Marley and Marley • One More Sleep 'Til Christmas • Room in Your Heart • Scrooge • Thankful Heart • When Love Is Gone.

00312483...$16.99

Tim Burton's The Nightmare Before Christmas

This book features 11 songs from Tim Burton's creepy animated classic, with music and lyrics by Danny Elfman. Songs include: Jack's Lament • Jack's Obsession • Kidnap the Sandy Claws • Making Christmas • Oogie Boogie's Song • Poor Jack • Sally's Song • This Is Halloween • Town Meeting Song • What's This? • Finale/Reprise.

00312488...$16.99

A Sentimental Christmas Book

An outstanding collection of nearly 30 beloved Christmas favorites, including: All I Want for Christmas Is You • Blue Christmas • Christmas Lights • The Christmas Shoes • The Christmas Song (Chestnuts Roasting on an Open Fire) • Christmas Time Is Here • Christmases When You Were Mine • Fairytale of New York • Grown-Up Christmas List • Have Yourself a Merry Little Christmas • (There's No Place Like) Home for the Holidays • I'll Be Home for Christmas • Please Come Home for Christmas • Silver Bells • Somewhere in My Memory • Where Are You Christmas? • White Christmas • You're All I Want for Christmas • and more.

00236830...$14.99

Ultimate Christmas – 3rd Edition

100 seasonal favorites: Auld Lang Syne • Bring a Torch, Jeannette, Isabella • Carol of the Bells • The Chipmunk Song • Christmas Time Is Here • The First Noel • Frosty the Snow Man • Gesù Bambino • Happy Holiday • Happy Xmas (War Is Over) • Hymne • Jesu, Joy of Man's Desiring • Jingle-Bell Rock • March of the Toys • My Favorite Things • The Night Before Christmas Song • Pretty Paper • Silver and Gold • Silver Bells • Suzy Snowflake • What Child Is This • The Wonderful World of Christmas • and more.

00361399 ....$22.99

THE ULTIMATE SONGBOOKS

HAL•LEONARD®
PIANO PLAY-ALONG

These great songbook/audio packs come with our standard arrangements for piano and voice with guitar chord frames plus audio. The audio includes a full performance of each song, as well as a second track without the piano part so you can play "lead" with the band!

BOOK/CD PACKS

No.	Title	Item	Price
1.	**Movie Music**	00311072	$14.95
7.	**Love Songs**	00311078	$14.95
12.	**Christmas Favorites**	00311137	$15.95
15.	**Favorite Standards**	00311146	$14.95
27.	**Andrew Lloyd Webber Greats**	00311179	$14.95
28.	**Lennon & McCartney**	00311180	$14.95
29.	**The Beach Boys**	00311181	$14.95
31.	**Carpenters**	00311183	$17.99
44.	**Frank Sinatra – Popular Hits**	00311277	$14.95
45.	**Frank Sinatra – Most Requested Songs**	00311278	$14.95
53.	**Grease**	00311450	$14.95
64.	**God Bless America**	00311489	$14.95
71.	**George Gershwin**	00102687	$24.99
72.	**Van Morrison**	00103053	$14.99
77.	**Elton John Favorites**	00311884	$14.99
78.	**Eric Clapton**	00311885	$14.99
81.	**Josh Groban**	00311901	$14.99
82.	**Lionel Richie**	00311902	$14.99
86.	**Barry Manilow**	00311935	$14.99
87.	**Patsy Cline**	00311936	$14.99
90.	**Irish Favorites**	00311969	$14.99
92.	**Disney Favorites**	00311973	$14.99
97.	**Great Classical Themes**	00312020	$14.99
98.	**Christmas Cheer**	00312021	$14.99
103.	**Gospel Favorites**	00312044	$14.99
105.	**Bee Gees**	00312055	$14.99
106.	**Carole King**	00312056	$14.99
107.	**Bob Dylan**	00312057	$14.99
108.	**Simon & Garfunkel**	00312058	$14.99
114.	**Motown**	00312176	$14.99
115.	**John Denver**	00312249	$14.99
123.	**Chris Tomlin**	00312563	$14.99
125.	**Katy Perry**	00109373	$14.99

BOOKS/ONLINE AUDIO

No.	Title	Item	Price
5.	**Disney**	00311076	$14.99
8.	**The Piano Guys – Uncharted**	00202549	$24.99
9.	**The Piano Guys – Christmas Together**	00259567	$24.99
16.	**Coldplay**	00316506	$16.99
20.	**La La Land**	00241591	$19.99
24.	**Les Misérables**	00311169	$14.99
25.	**The Sound of Music**	00311175	$15.99
30.	**Elton John Hits**	00311182	$16.99
32.	**Adele**	00156222	$24.99
33.	**Peanuts™**	00311227	$14.99
34.	**A Charlie Brown Christmas**	00311228	$16.99
46.	**Wicked**	00311317	$16.99
62.	**Billy Joel Hits**	00311465	$14.99
65.	**Casting Crowns**	00311494	$14.99
69.	**Pirates of the Caribbean**	00311807	$15.99
73.	**Mamma Mia! – The Movie**	00311831	$15.99
76.	**Pride & Prejudice**	00311862	$15.99
83.	**Phantom of the Opera**	00311903	$15.99
113.	**Queen**	00312164	$16.99
117.	**Alicia Keys**	00312306	$17.99
118.	**Adele**	00312307	$14.99
126.	**Bruno Mars**	00123121	$14.99
127.	**Star Wars**	00110282	$14.99
128.	**Frozen**	00126480	$16.99
130.	**West Side Story**	00130738	$14.99
131.	**The Piano Guys – Wonders** 00141503 (Contains backing tracks only)		$24.99

HAL•LEONARD®

7777 W. BLUEMOUND RD. P.O. BOX 13819 MILWAUKEE, WI 53213

Order online from your favorite music retailer at
halleonard.com

0820
276

PLAY PIANO LIKE A PRO!

AMAZING PHRASING – KEYBOARD
50 Ways to Improve Your Improvisational Skills
by Debbie Denke

Amazing Phrasing is for any keyboard player interested in learning how to improvise and how to improve their creative phrasing. This method is divided into three parts: melody, harmony, and rhythm & style. The online audio contains 44 full-band demos for listening, as well as many play-along examples so you can practice improvising over various musical styles and progressions.
00842030 Book/Online Audio.. $16.99

BEBOP LICKS FOR PIANO
A Dictionary of Melodic Ideas for Improvisation
by Les Wise

Written for the musician who is interested in acquiring a firm foundation for playing jazz, this unique book/audio pack presents over 800 licks. By building up a vocabulary of these licks, players can connect them together in endless possibilities to form larger phrases and complete solos. The book includes piano notation, and the online audio contains helpful note-for-note demos of every lick.
00311854 Book/Online Audio.. $17.99

BOOGIE WOOGIE FOR BEGINNERS
by Frank Paparelli

A short easy method for learning to play boogie woogie, designed for the beginner and average pianist. Includes: exercises for developing left-hand bass • 25 popular boogie woogie bass patterns • arrangements of "Down the Road a Piece" and "Answer to the Prayer" by well-known pianists • a glossary of musical terms for dynamics, tempo and style.
00120517 .... $10.99

HAL LEONARD JAZZ PIANO METHOD
by Mark Davis

This is a comprehensive and easy-to-use guide designed for anyone interested in playing jazz piano – from the complete novice just learning the basics to the more advanced player who wishes to enhance their keyboard vocabulary. The accompanying audio includes demonstrations of all the examples in the book! Topics include essential theory, chords and voicings, improvisation ideas, structure and forms, scales and modes, rhythm basics, interpreting a lead sheet, playing solos, and much more!
00131102 Book/Online Audio.. $19.99

INTROS, ENDINGS & TURNAROUNDS FOR KEYBOARD
Essential Phrases for Swing, Latin, Jazz Waltz, and Blues Styles
by John Valerio

Learn the intros, endings and turnarounds that all of the pros know and use! This new keyboard instruction book by John Valerio covers swing styles, ballads, Latin tunes, jazz waltzes, blues, major and minor keys, vamps and pedal tones, and more.
00290525 .... $12.99

JAZZ PIANO TECHNIQUE
Exercises, Etudes & Ideas for Building Chops
by John Valerio

This one-of-a-kind book applies traditional technique exercises to specific jazz piano needs. Topics include: scales (major, minor, chromatic, pentatonic, etc.), arpeggios (triads, seventh chords, upper structures), finger independence exercises (static position, held notes, Hanon exercises), parallel interval scales and exercises (thirds, fourths, tritones, fifths, sixths, octaves), and more! The online audio includes 45 recorded examples.
00312059 Book/Online Audio.. $19.99

JAZZ PIANO VOICINGS
An Essential Resource for Aspiring Jazz Musicians
by Rob Mullins

The jazz idiom can often appear mysterious and difficult for musicians who were trained to play other types of music. Long-time performer and educator Rob Mullins helps players enter the jazz world by providing voicings that will help the player develop skills in the jazz genre and start sounding professional right away – without years of study! Includes a "Numeric Voicing Chart," chord indexes in all 12 keys, info about what range of the instrument you can play chords in, and a beginning approach to bass lines.
00310914 .... $19.99

OSCAR PETERSON – JAZZ EXERCISES, MINUETS, ETUDES & PIECES FOR PIANO

Legendary jazz pianist Oscar Peterson has long been devoted to the education of piano students. In this book he offers dozens of pieces designed to empower the student, whether novice or classically trained, with the technique needed to become an accomplished jazz pianist.
00311225 .... $14.99

PIANO AEROBICS
by Wayne Hawkins

Piano Aerobics is a set of exercises that introduces students to many popular styles of music, including jazz, salsa, swing, rock, blues, new age, gospel, stride, and bossa nova. In addition, there is a online audio with accompaniment tracks featuring professional musicians playing in those styles.
00311863 Book/Online Audio $19.99

PIANO FITNESS
A Complete Workout
by Mark Harrison

This book will give you a thorough technical workout, while having fun at the same time! The accompanying online audio allows you to play along with a rhythm section as you practice your scales, arpeggios, and chords in all keys. Instead of avoiding technique exercises because they seem too tedious or difficult, you'll look forward to playing them. Various voicings and rhythmic settings, which are extremely useful in a variety of pop and jazz styles, are also introduced.
00311995 Book/Online Audio.. $19.99

HAL•LEONARD®
7777 W. BLUEMOUND RD. P.O. BOX 13819
MILWAUKEE, WISCONSIN 53213
www.halleonard.com

Prices, contents, and availability subject to change without notice.